American Attempt to Take Canada

War of 1812 – 1814

St. Joseph Island - Mackinac Island

Sault Ste. Marie

Updated Second Edition

Sandra Rousseau

Revised April, 2018

Published by Awaken Ink Inc. 2018
Sault Ste. Marie, Ontario

ISBN 978-1-989142-19-6

HMS Nancy on front cover
Illustration by Peter Rindlisbacher contained in *Legion Canada's Military History Magazine*, February 5, 2013.

Reviews

"Sandra Rousseau's *American Attempt to Take Canada, War of 1812 – 1814* is a lively and fascinating history of a neglected part of the War of 1812, namely the struggle between Canada and the U.S. in the upper Lake Huron region. The author presents detailed accounts of military actions in the region as well as background on the soldiers, sailors, fur traders, and Native participants. I highly recommend this book for those interested in Canadian and upper Great Lakes history and biography."

- **Dr. W. Stephen McBride, Camp Nelson Civil War Heritage Park and McBride Preservations Services**

"I encountered Sandra Rousseau several years ago while researching for a novel set in the time of the famous 1812 attack on Fort Michilimackinac. Her apparent grasp of the subject was so complete, I was compelled to contact her directly and profited greatly from the ensuing association. Ms. Rousseau has now expanded on her research in an easy to read monograph that puts to rest any doubt about the intentions of the Americans or the resolve of the Canadians before and during that conflict.

The background leading to the war is set out in clarity. I liked the way she breathes life into the major players, particularly Robert Dickson, John Askew, Captain Charles Roberts. Her treatment of these and others populating the fur trade routes, make the reading of history come alive.

Rousseau tends to examine events from more than

one aspect, there being those of the Americans, the English Canadians, the French, and the Natives. She explains the importance of the fur trade to all sides, particularly the Americans who needed the fort on Mackinac Island to assure trade route superiority. Her treatment of the preparations for and the actual attack by the Canadians and Ojibwa from St. Joseph Island is not the first to be written but is told in clear context. I don't believe an interested reader will find a more thorough or personal rendering of this subject.
For anyone interested in the war if 1812, I highly recommend Sandra Rousseau's well-written treatment."
-Richard Whitten Barnes, Author of Mysteries and Historical Fiction. **New for 2018 MEDALLION**

"In Canada, much of the attention of the bicentenary of the War of 1812 is limited to a few regions, most notably, the Niagara Peninsula. It is often forgotten that the North West encompassed a vast area that witnessed a number of important actions; the American Attempt to Take Canada examines, in general terms, the wartime events at St. Joseph Island, Mackinac Island, Sault Ste. Marie and naval events in Georgian Bay. By no means a scholarly study, this . . . is a fine example of local history, and provides a good introduction to the war in (the) area around Sault Ste. Marie."
-Major John R. Grodzinski, CD, BA, Ma, PhD, Assistant Professor, Dept. of History, Royal Military College of Canada. Review of first edition *American Attempt to Take Canada: War of 1812 – 1814*, in the War of 1812 Magazine, Issue 19, December, 2012.

Table of Contents

Map 6
Prelude to War 1
Captain Charles Roberts 7
John Askin, Jr. 9
Who Got the Word Out? 11
Official Declaration 13
Too Quiet on Mackinac Island 17
Canadians Attack Mackinac Island 19
Beautiful St. Joe 28
Destruction of Fort St. Joseph 30
Sidetracked 32
Burning the Sault 34
Assessing the Damage at the Sault 39
Fur Brigade 41
Battle of Mackinac Island 1814 44
US Brig *Niagara* 50
Map – The Northern Theatre of War 52
Map Nottawasaga River 58
Flour to the Rescue 59
Trouble on the Horizon 61
Revenge by Batteaux 63
Scorpion Attack 65
Treaty of Ghent 68
Effects of the Treaty of Ghent 69
The Upshot 71
Where Did the Defenders Go? 75
About the Author 86
Ermatinger-Clergue National Historic Site 88
Endnotes 89
Bibliography 91

Map

Partial map of major war areas.
Ermatinger-Clergue National Historic Site

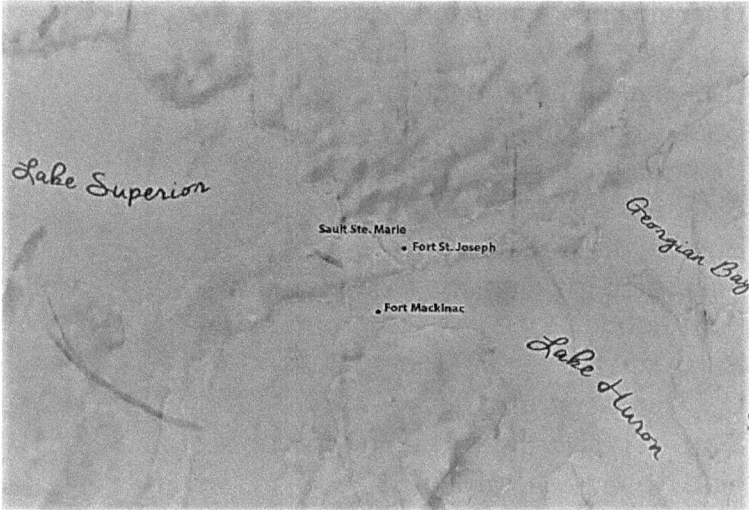

Lake Superior

Sault Ste. Marie
• Fort St. Joseph

• Fort Mackinac

Georgian Bay

Lake Huron

Major-General Sir Isaac Brock

stated in February, 1812:

"….unless Detroit and Michilimackinac

be both in our possession at the

commencement of hostilities,

not only Amherstburg

but most probably

the whole country,

must be evacuated

as far as Kingston."

"A Mere Matter of Marching," confidently stated the former U.S. President Thomas Jefferson regarding the planned U.S.A. attack on Canada, in 1812. It was logical for him to make such a remark considering that Canada had about 300,000 inhabitants, while the U.S. had a population of more than 7.5 million.

The Canadian General, Isaac Brock, had a feeling that the Americans would soon be up to something, so he was anxious to get a message to Robert Dickson.

Where was Dickson?

His fur trading areas were Michigan, Wisconsin, Iowa, Minnesota, and South Dakota. I can picture Brock emphatically stating to his next in command, "get ahold of that red-headed Scotsman!"

Dickson, called Mascotopah, by the Sioux, in recognition of his hair and beard, of a fiery colour, had the respect of the Natives. He would encourage them to muster for Canada which would tip the balance of power. He just had to find him!

At over six feet in height, it would not be a problem to spot him, but it was not known exactly where Dickson was. There was some thought that he was living with the Natives in the Missouri area. Two couriers, in an express canoe, were dispatched in that direction. It took about four months, but Brock's urgent message was handed to Dickson when he was discovered near what is today Portage, Wisconsin.

Robert Dickson

As it turned out, Dickson received Brock's letter on the very day that the U.S. declared war. He sent a response the same day, being June 18, 1812, basically stating that he had many Native friends who would help defend Canada.

Dickson, at the age of 21 years, had got his start in the fur trade at Michilimackinac Island, in July, 1786. With his likeable personality, coupled with his honesty, he became a very successful trader.

At some point during his travels, he met Totowin, known as Helen to English speakers. She was a medicine woman whose father was an important chief of the Wahpeton band of the Santee Sioux of South Dakota. In 1797, they married, creating an admirable partnership.

By nature, native wives were hardworking assets to their husbands, so it was no surprise that, in the course of rallying support for the British, Totowin worked diligently alongside her husband.

Being Canadian, there developed trading problems for Dickson following Jays Treaty of 1794, involving heavy customs duties on Canadian goods. So, partly due to his British ancestry, partly because he despised how the Americans treated the Natives, and partly due to business concerns, he was more than happy to secure support for Canada to repel an attack on it by the Americans.

With a Native alliance, there would be no stopping the Canadians.

Dickson and Totowin gathered warriors together in record time and set out for the British fort on St. Joseph Island, Ontario, situated between northern Lake Huron and the St. Marys River. ("St. Marys" is not grammatically correct, but that is just how it came to be.)

By the standards of the time, it was a quick paddle by canoe from Fort St. Joseph to Michilimackinac Island, which, at that time, was normally referred to as Mackinaw, although it was spelled Mackinac. I will refer to it as Mackinac Island, which is what it is presently named.

It would be a brilliant feat to take over Mackinac Island because it was located between Lakes Huron and Michigan, which would provide a natural defence of the Canadian upper Great Lakes country.

From there, it would be only a matter of time before Detroit could be seized as well.

The Natives were relied upon to trap the furs, and

Canada's economy was the fur trade.

The people living on St. Joseph Island were traders who had business, as well as personal, contacts with the Natives and fur traders throughout a vast area. Therefore, the setting on St. Joseph Island was conducive to rallying against the American threat of war.

John Askin Jr was the storekeeper for the government Indian Department on St. Joseph Island. Probably because his mother was Native, he had a close relationship with the Natives.

Charles Langlade, Jr, another interpreter, was living there. Incidentally, Langlade, Jr. had been raised on Mackinac Island, and educated in Montreal. He held the position of Ensign in the British Indian Department and had moved to St. Joseph Island when the British vacated Mackinac Island in 1796.

My ancestor, Jean Baptiste Rousseau, and his brother, Charles, were both there as clerks for their half-brother, George Gordon, who was at Michipicoten as a clerk for the Northwest Company.

Gordon dropped what he was doing and paddled to St. Joseph Island, upon hearing the news of war.

They all had business interests and trade goods on Mackinac Island.

My great-great-great-great grandfather, Dominique Rousseau of Montreal, father of Jean Baptiste and Charles, owned real estate on Mackinac Island, and through others, including Dickson and Toussaint Pothier, conducted business there as a supplier of goods and as a fur trader. He was very likely on Mackinac Island, at this time, as it was his custom to spend his summers there. He was a Major in the militia at Montreal but, at age 57 years, may have sat out this conflict.

The St. Joseph Islanders were friends with the people on Mackinac Island. They were neighbours. There were marriages between them. The defence of their own Island was paramount, but with assets, business interests, friends, and family on Mackinac Island, there had to be a way of taking that island, without severe damage.

Étienne-Augustin Rocbert de la Morandière, who was also my great-great-great-great grandfather, had been a fur trader and clerk for John Jacob Astor, since 1784.

By 1805, he was living on Mackinac Island which was the headquarters for Astor's business. Traders obtained goods for trading from the headquarters, but the pelts that were purchased from the Natives during the winter were shipped to the various trading posts, one of which was established by Rocbert de la Morandière at Muskegon.

Étienne and Sai-Sai-Go-No-Kwe (Woman of Falling Snow) had various children who were born on Mackinac Island. The entire family was there except for Étienne who had gone to St. Joseph Island in anticipation of war.

By the time the war started, Étienne held the rank of Ensign for the British.

The mere whisper of war would have put the garrison at Fort St. Joseph on high alert.

It was the most westerly British garrison in Canada, with Captain Charles Roberts as its commander.

Captain Charles Roberts

Roberts had been in the British army since 1795. There are reports that he had spent his first ten years of service in India and Ceylon (now known as Sri Lanka). Other reports placed his first decade of service mainly in Trinidad.

His health was precarious in that he suffered from ongoing fever as well as severe gastric and intestinal problems. Due to his compromised health, he sought a veteran battalion, thinking that it would not be physically demanding.

In 1811, he was chosen to command the Tenth Royal Veteran Battalion at Fort St. Joseph. As it was a veteran battalion, the soldiers were not in their prime. In fact, most of them suffered from alcoholism.

Really, they were there simply to garrison the fort, which was established in 1796, after the Canadians had left Fort Michilimackinac, on Mackinac Island. The soldiers at Fort St. Joseph had no expectation of actual warfare because this fort was merely intended to protect the fur trade and to foster goodwill with the Natives.

Although Roberts was not at his physical best, it can be said that he did the utmost that anyone could have done, given the scant resources at hand. For example, when he took over command, his men were wearing threadbare winter coats. Roberts requisitioned new coats, but none arrived. By November of 1811, he knew that no replacement coats were going to arrive for the coming winter.

Ingenuity was one of his strong points in that he obtained more than forty 3 ½ point Hudson's Bay blankets, which were the more expensive type of blankets, from John Askin Jr. at the King's Store. Only after he had arranged for the blankets, did Roberts write to advise his superior officer that he had acquired all those blankets that had been meant for the Natives in exchange for valuable furs.

Without a minute's delay, Madelaine, presumed wife of Askin Jr. arranged for a group of women, of mixed heritage, to create what some call a blanket coat. The women gathered together in the King's Store and had all of the greatcoats completed within two weeks.

A year later, the coat became known as a Mackinac, because Roberts had to go through the same procedure of having coats made at Mackinac Island.

The name has stuck for a very long time. As a kid, I can remember my father telling me, "get your mackinac on!" At the time I had no idea that my favourite coat was as a result of Captain Roberts' ingenuity.

John Askin, Jr.

There is a discrepancy about John Askin Jr. in that Madelaine was noted in numerous articles, as being his wife. In April, 2018, I was horrified to learn that two historical authors provided a quote that confirms that Madelaine was not his wife.

George S. May quoted Askin, Jr. in *War 1812*, which was published in the U.S. between 1923 and 1963. Frank Straus also quoted Askin, Jr. in an article in the Mackinac Island Town Crier, on May 17, 2014, about Captain Richard Bullock, entitled *Forgotten Army Captain Left Legacy on Mackinac Island.*

Bullock replaced Captain Charles Roberts, on Mackinac Island, on September 14, 1813, and was there until replaced by Lieutenant Colonel Robert McDouall, on May 18, 1814.

Both authors made reference to a quote made by Askin, Jr. in a letter to his son in October, 1813. The quote by Askin, Jr. was: "My negro wench, Madelaine, absconded two days ago and I am just informed that Captain Bullock has taken her into his service – he must be a damn scoundrel. I told him that she was my slave and that all those born before 1793 are slaves."

Although many credible writers described a woman, known as Madeline, as his wife, based on this quote, Madeline was actually his black slave.

Askin Jr.'s mother was an Ottawa Native named Manette or Monette. She had been a slave who was purchased by Askin, Sr. from M. Bourassa at Mackinac Island. Askin, Sr. freed her in 1766. Well, he freed her enough to give birth to his first three

9

children, one of which was John, Jr. who likely was born between 1762 and 1765, as well as two girls, named Catherine and Madelaine.

Askin, Jr. had previously fought in the U.S. against the settlers who were trying to take land from the Natives. I was very surprised to read that he had fought at the Battle of Fallen Timbers in 1794.

The Battle of Fallen Timbers, on August 20, 1794, is well known in U.S. history and documented as the final battle of the Northwestern Indian Wars. A young Tecumseh, the Shawnee leader Blue Jacket, the Ottawa chief Me-sa-sa (called Turkey Foot by the non-natives) along with his son, all fought in this battle. Me-sa-sa, who was my 5th great-grandfather, was one of the main battle leaders. Me-sa-sa was shot and killed when he leaped onto a three-foot high boulder to rally the warriors. The boulder is now a historical marker known as Turkey Foot Rock which is situated at the base of Presque Isle Hill, beside the Maumee River, in northwestern Ohio.

Staying true blue to the British, Askin, Jr. returned to the Upper Canada soon after this battle.

By 1807, he was appointed as the storekeeper for the Indian Department at Fort St. Joseph on St. Joseph Island, Ontario. Then, as we know he took part in the war of 1812 – 1814.

Me-sa-sa, Jr. (also known as Turkey Foot, Jr.) and Tecumseh were both killed on October 5, 1813 in the Battle of the Thames, at Moraviantown, near Chatham, Ontario.

Who Got the Word Out?

Roberts' first clue that war was imminent must have been when Dickson arrived with his Natives on June 30, although at this point neither man had received word that war had been declared.

Joseph Tasse in his book, written in 1878, entitled *Les Canadiens de l'Ouest*, at page 148, stated that at receiving the news of the war, on *July 4,* Roberts consulted with Toussaint Pothier, Northwest Company agent, as to what they should do but did not explain that his plan was to make an immediate attack on Mackinac Island.

Tasse also wrote that this intrepid Canadian [Pothier] promised Roberts his active help.

There are reports that Pothier travelled to the Island to give Roberts the news of war, but this reference is clear that Pothier was already on the island, so that it was Roberts who gave the news to Pothier.

William McKay, a retired Northwest fur trade partner, who was living in Montreal, said that when he received confirmation that war had been declared, he immediately left for St. Joseph Island to deliver the news. Some reports say that he was the messenger for the Governor General and other reports state that he carried the message from General Brock.

McKay stated that he arrived within eight days which would have put him on the Island on July 2, although this date is not in accordance with July 4 as stated by Tasse. In fact, Tasse did not even mention McKay but I wonder if that was due to a French focus

11

only.

As mentioned by Jean Morrison in *Superior Rendezvous Place, Fort William in the Canadian Fur Trade*, on pages 73 and 74, William McKay left Quebec on June 25 for Fort St. Joseph and then proceeded on to Fort William, now known as Thunder Bay, to advise members of the Northwest Company of the war.

The Northwest Company personnel then went into fervent overtime in an effort to get furs ready to be transported to Montreal. To accomplish this, Archibald McLellan quickly went to what is now Rainy Lake to supervise getting the furs out of the upper country and, at the same time, to gather together Natives who would assist in getting the furs safely on their way to the mouth of the French River, on Georgian Bay. Others set out for Sault Ste. Marie with a view to protecting their assets there while those who were meant to assist Roberts got ready to leave.

Official Declaration

When Governor General Sir George Prevost, in Québec, received official communication that the Congress of the United States of America had declared war on Great Britain, he sent a letter to Roberts, instructing him to act defensively, to protect the Northwest Company.

Upon the Governor of Upper Canada, General Brock, being advised of the declaration, he sent a letter via messenger to Roberts, advising him to get ready to attack Mackinac Island immediately.

There was a valid reason for this. If the Americans were to continue holding Mackinac Island, they would be in a good position to capture the furs passing through Sault Ste. Marie, on their way to the French River. This would cripple the Canadian economy.

Bayliss, in *Historic St. Joseph Island*, at page 55, wrote a comical fact about this letter from Brock. It was franked by the Secretary of the American Treasury. I could not determine why the letter from a Canadian to another Canadian was franked by an American but I seem to recall that the mail passed through Michigan at that time to get to the area of the Sault. It was just one of those quirky things that happened.

Then Brock had to get a message to Roberts to defer his attack against Mackinac Island because Prevost had decided that a quick settlement of the issues could be attained.

With no quick settlement in sight, Brock sent his

third command, on July 4, advising Roberts to proceed as he saw fit.

Meanwhile, when Roberts was handed the first letter (whether it was July 2, 4 or 8, we cannot be sure) he had already started to get ready for his offence. He had forty regular soldiers and four officers, but he had a major problem in that his soldiers were not fit enough for warfare.

He knew that the garrison at Mackinac Island had fifty-seven to sixty-one men, with two being officers, led by its commander, Lieutenant Porter Hanks, so that he was somewhat outnumbered.

Fran Robb, a seasoned presenter at Fort St. Joseph, mentioned to me that many of the American soldiers at Mackinac suffered from scurvy. I do not know if Roberts knew about the scurvy concern, but I suspect that he likely was aware of it.

Ultimately, it was going to be up to the Canadians, being the clerks, fur traders, and voyageurs, as well as the Natives, to fight the battle.

Chief Shingwauk, or Shingwaukonse, also known as Little Pine, and the Crane chiefs of Sault Ste. Marie had previously attended a council on Mackinac Island, in 1808, to discuss if they would join the British in any potential hostilities with the Americans, and their decision was positive.

Shingwaukonse was trading at Fort William when he received word that war was imminent. He returned immediately to join under the command of his nephew, John Askin Jr.

Later, the local Natives who had mustered for the attack against Mackinac fought with Brock against Detroit.

Shingwaukonse was definitely at the battle at Queenston Heights, and legend tells us that he was the one who killed the man who shot General Isacc Brock at this battle.

He may also have fought at Prairie du Chien, Lundy's Lane, and the area around Lake Erie.

It must have been an incredibly heartwarming scene for Roberts to witness the expansion of his troops within such a brief period.

Dickson arrived, as mentioned above, on June 30, along with his friends, being fifty-six Sioux, forty-eight Winnebago, and thirty-nine Menominee, all with their chiefs.

As a result of communications by John Askin Jr., Charles Langlade, Jr, and Michel Cadotte, Jr. of Sault, Michigan, a group of about 300 Ojibway, Chippewa and Ottawa/Odawa Natives arrived.

John Johnston, who just happened to be the collector of U.S. government port taxes at Sault, Michigan, promptly arrived on St. Joseph Island to join the anticipated fray. Accompanying him were his sons and more Natives.

Tasse stated that Pothier added 160 to 260 French Canadian voyageurs to the mix, recruited by him from the Northwest Company, all of whom reported for duty immediately. Some reports state that they were all on St. Joe by July 3.

Tasse further explained that the Canadians were divided into three companies with Lewis Crawford appointed as Lieutenant-Colonel, Robert Livingston as Adjutant, Pothier as Major, and Joseph Rolette, Joseph Porier, Paul Lacroix and Xavier Biron as Lieutenants. From the Sault, were appointed three

Captains, namely, Jean Baptiste Nolin, John Johnston, and Charles Oakes Ermatinger. Leading the Natives were Robert Dickson as Lieutenant-Colonel, along with John Askin Jr., Charles Langlade, Jr. and Michel Cadot, Jr.

As it turned out, Nolin, who was age 70 years, did not take part due to illness, but his two sons, Louis and Augustin, joined the Ojibway warriors. In due course, Augustin Nolin was commended for his part in leading the Ojibways.

The garrison had expanded to about three hundred French and English and perhaps more than five hundred Natives. There is another report that states that there were four hundred Canadians and eight hundred Natives. In any event, it was far more than the forty-four that Roberts had anticipated.

If he had not been confident about his proposed attack the previous week, he must have felt ecstatic now. It was incredible that so many men came together, so quickly, for Canada.

They were about to head out into Lake Huron when the second communication arrived from Brock on July 12. What a letdown to the men who were pumped for action!

Now, the only problem was how to feed them all.

Too Quiet on Mackinac Island

When Lieutenant Hanks noticed that the Natives were leaving Mackinac Island, he wanted to know what was up.

Upon discussion with the Ottawa chief, See-gee-noe, no information was obtained.

Still, Hanks had to wonder.

He then had a meeting with his two officers and the American fur traders who were present on Mackinac.

The main trader was Michael Dousman, who was also Captain of the local Militia, but Canadians were his fur trade associates.

He, too, wondered what was going on because he knew that two of his agents, William Aitken and John Drew, had arrived at the Sault after trading around Lake Superior, but had not come to Mackinac.

As was the circumstance for many, Dousman owned property on St. Joseph Island. For this reason, it was decided that he should be the one to go there to check out what was happening.

At about sunset, on July 16, 1812, Dousman set out in his canoe, enjoying a peaceful journey, without a care in the world, while heading for St. Joseph Island.

Map of Mackinac Island

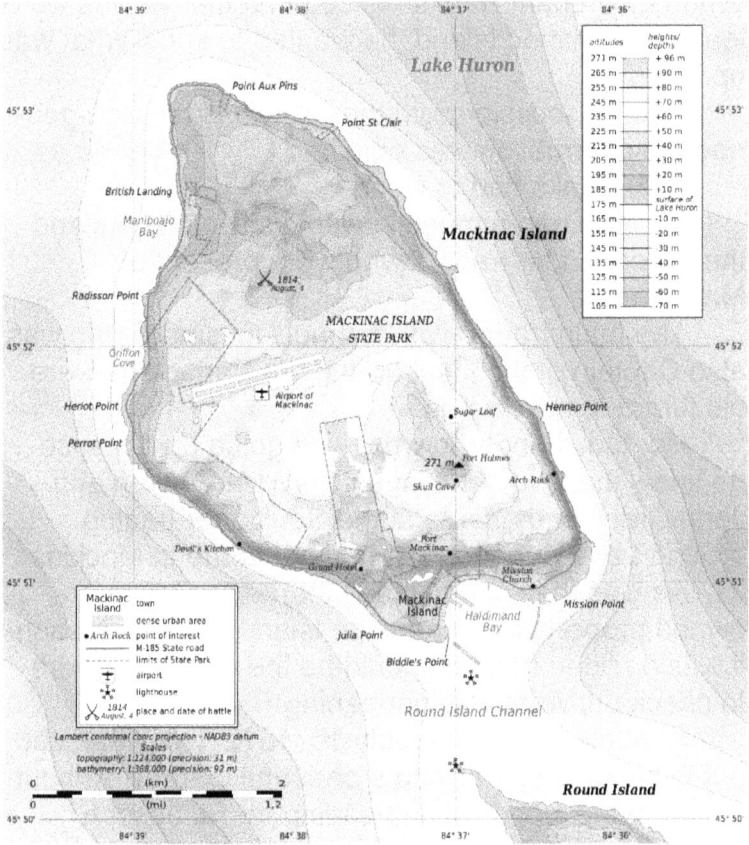

Canadians Attack Mackinac Island

Brock's third message arrived on July 15, 1812.

At 10:00 a.m. the following day, Roberts, with his soldiers and ragtag militia, set out for Mackinac Island.

I think it must have been an amazing assembly to view. The British soldiers led the way, in their red coats, with fife and drum marching them along the wharf, with flags flying. Next, the fur traders marched along with determination. They were followed by the voyageurs, dressed in their usual style of capotes, sashes, kerchiefs, and moccasins. Last, but most certainly not least, were the Natives in their full battledress.

The fur trade companies present donated to the cause their boats, including the Caledonia, which was a brig owned by the Northwest Company, two brass six-pounders, and their complete stock of guns and ammunition.

The Caledonia carried the soldiers, clerks, and fur traders, while the voyageurs and Natives travelled in ten batteaux and not less than seventy canoes.

The Caledonia

Fifteen miles (25 km) into his journey, Dousman paddled right into the midst of the Canadians, becoming their first prisoner of war.

Roberts had a great fear that the civilians at Mackinac could all be killed once the battle began. Trying to avoid a slaughter, he decided to send a British trader, named Oliver, to quietly awaken the civilians and direct them to a safe location.

Dousman was concerned that the residents might not believe someone who was unknown to them, so he requested that he go with Oliver, promising the Canadians that he would not inform the garrison about the impending military attack.

Dousman and Oliver then proceeded to Mackinac alone.

Upon arrival, Dousman aroused Ambrose Davenport, explained what was happening, and secured his promise that he would keep quiet about the matter.

With Davenport's help, the residents were awakened and directed to safety in the south-west side of the Island, close to the old distillery, which Roberts had ordered to be guarded, presumably by Oliver.

In the meantime, the flotilla continued during the night toward Mackinac, landing at 3:00 a.m. on July 17, at a location on the north-west side of the Island, known thereafter as British Landing. It took some effort, but with the use of Dousman's oxen, a cannon was pulled up to a height of 318 feet (96.92 meters) from Lake Huron to a position overlooking the fort

By 9:00 a.m., everything was organized for the attack to begin at 10:00 a.m.

Dr. Sylvester Day, a surgeon at the post, who was awakened by the movements of people, investigated and then decided to go to see Hanks to divulge what he had seen.

Before Day arrived, Hanks woke up and realized that there was dead silence all around the village.

He then sent Lieutenant Archibald Darragh and two other men to find out why the place was so quiet.

At that same time, the Natives gave a threatening war-whoop.

With that, the entire garrison suddenly jumped into action!

Day then arrived, advising of his observations, and Hanks then knew there was definitely an attack underway. Hanks then ordered ammunition to be made ready in the blockhouses.

Meanwhile, over at the distillery, the sheltered people persuaded Davenport, Dousman, and others, named Samuel Abbott, Bostwick, and Stone, to go to the shore and give themselves up.

Dickson was standing on the shore to receive prisoners. When he was approached, he strongly advised the men to go to Hanks to urge him to surrender immediately to avoid any bloodshed.

With a flag of truce, Dousman, Abbott, and Davenport arrived at the fort at 11:30 a.m.

Hanks had no clue that his country had declared war on Britain.

Making the right decision for the people and assets that he was meant to protect, he agreed to the surrender terms, thus ending the first battle of the war, without a shot being fired.

How many battle commanders can make that claim?

Roberts must have felt immense relief, mixed with pride in the accomplishment.

The Articles of Capitulation, signed by Captain Roberts and Lieutenant Hanks, are set out in numerous references, but I have taken the clauses from *Historic St. Joseph Island* at page 62:

"The Fort of Michilimackinac shall immediately be surrendered to the British force;
The garrison shall march out with the honours of war, lay down their arms and become prisoners of war and shall be sent to the United States of America by His Britannic Majesty, not to serve this war until regularly exchanged, and for the due performance of this article the officers pledge their word of honour.
All the merchants' vessels in the harbour, with their cargoes, shall be in possession of their respective owners.
Private property shall be held sacred as far as in my [Captain Roberts'] power.
All citizens of the United States who shall not take the oath of allegiance of His Britannic Majesty shall depart with their property from the island in one month from the date hereof."

The purpose of the second clause was to avoid prisoner of war camps, which was the normal procedure in this war. The captured men were to return to their homes until such time as both sides met to exchange prisoners of war.

Regarding the fifth clause, most of the residents of Mackinac Island had no problem swearing allegiance to Britain because many of them had been British in the past, as this was not the first time in recent history that the island had changed hands. For them, it was a matter of swearing allegiance and getting on with their day.

The participants on behalf of the British were later financially compensated by their government, but in the meantime, the spoils of war were enjoyed by one and all, and there was something for everyone on the British side. All kinds of provisions from the fort were divided up among the victors, including copious amounts of wine and rum.

Had anyone wanted to attack the fort that night, it might have been a hard decision whether to fight it out or party hardy.

Two days after the capture of Mackinac Island, the Northwest contingent from Fort William arrived; fortunately, they had not been needed for this attack.

The paroled Americans were escorted to Detroit by Lieutenant Robert R. Livingston of the Indian Department on St. Joseph Island.

Upon arriving there on August 4, Livingston discovered that not every military officer was logical given the American General, William Hull, refused to acknowledge the executed Articles of Capitulation.

Hull promptly ordered the paroled prisoners of war into his service.

Lieutenant Hanks, who had been most honourable at Mackinac, was killed when a British cannon struck him on August 16, 1812.

Hull, being terrified about the number of Natives on the British side, signed Articles of Capitulation that same day, putting Detroit into Brock's domain.

Actually, the Canadian General had tricked Hull into believing that there were far more Natives involved in the attack than there really were, which Pierre Berton described in his book, *The Capture of Detroit* on pages 105 and 106.

Tecumseh, under Brock's direction, had his warriors make their way across a field, into the thick trees, out again, and across the field again. Around

they went several times, doing what it took to
seemingly outnumber the enemy.
    But that's another story!

Natives on the Attack on Mackinac Island
After two weeks on Mackinac Island, Dickson and his
Native friends left.
Illustration by Dirk Gringhuis. www.warof1812-
bicentennial.info

Reenactors at Mackinac Island.

www.crazycrow.com/site/event/fort-michilimackinac-reenactment-pageant/

Photo of Re-enactment of British soldiers 1812 at
Ermatinger-Clergue National Historic Site
old.stone.house@cityssm.on.ca

Beautiful St. Joe

There was a major difference between Mackinac Island and St. Joseph Island. Mackinac had rocky terrain, making it difficult to practice agriculture, whereas St. Joseph was a beautiful, bountiful garden.

John Askin Jr. wrote to his father, in 1810, about the attributes of St. Joseph Island that he compared with Sandwich, now Windsor.

He described how a man could live so much better on St. Joseph Island and could acquire all the necessities, as well as the luxuries, of life for his family, and then went on to list the benefits.

Hares, partridges, ducks, bears, reindeer, and fish of superior quality, were all available.

There was no shortage of food because the fertile soil provided as many vegetables from his own garden as his family could possibly consume.

His property produced plenty of wild hay to provide for his cattle throughout the winter.

He owned four cows, one ox, two horses, and numerous hogs.

More than enough wood was stacked in his yard, which had been cut from an abundance of trees on his property, to keep his four fireplaces blazing.

Wine and spirits arrived by regular ship service, for little cost.

His neighbours were social, enjoying cards, dances, and dinners.

He summed up by saying that the money he earned enabled him to keep his family extremely well, with money left over for savings.

This ideal atmosphere came to an end with the capture of Mackinac because everyone from St. Joseph was required to move to Mackinac to defend it.

Fort St. Joseph 1812
www.uppercanadahistory.ca

Fort St. Joseph 1812

Destruction of Fort St. Joseph

On July 3, 1814, American ships set out from Detroit, arriving at St. Joseph Island on July 20. Once there, came the realization that the island had been deserted.

With no one present to defend, it was no contest as to the destruction of the fort by burning it to the ground.

In a letter, dated July 22, 1814, Captain Arthur Sinclair, on board the *Niagara*, near St. Joseph Island, wrote to the Secretary of the U.S. Navy, "The enemy had abandoned his work, consisting of a fort and a large block-house, etc.; those we destroyed but left untouched the town and Northwest Company's storehouses."[1]

I would like to know what "etc." represented.

Apart from that, I cannot imagine that he would have left the Northwest Company's storehouses unscathed. Other reports state that its storehouses were completely destroyed by fire.

Perhaps Sinclair was mistaken and actually meant to write that the South West Company storehouses, which were owned by the influential American, John Jacob Astor, were not torched.

The buildings of the fort were mainly built of stone, with sheet iron for the roofs, so there was not much chance of them going up in smoke, but there were other structures of wood.

Not all of the structures at the Fort were destroyed but by the end of the war, the Fort was dilapidated.

Fort St. Joseph National Historic Site – Parks Canada

Sidetracked

The Americans knew that they needed to sail to Mackinac Island, but their ships were unable to proceed there due to unfavourable winds.

While they were playing a waiting weather game, in the vicinity of St. Joseph Island, toward them sailed the *Mink*.

I cannot imagine the terror that the crew of this Northwest Company schooner felt when they spotted the six large American ships.

The *Mink* had been on its way from Mackinac to Sault Ste. Marie and, wind or no wind, the six American ships captured it.

From one of the prisoners of war taken from the *Mink*, they determined that it carried flour, which was meant to be transferred to the *Perseverance* at the Sault, to be transported to Fort William, (now Thunder Bay) Ontario.

The Americans decided that Major Holmes would take a party of regulars along with U.S. Navy Lieutenant Turner, aboard launches, to Sault Ste. Marie.

Their main aim there was to destroy the Northwest Company assets and starve the Nor'westers into surrendering. Seizing valuable furs was not going to do them any harm either. Then, capturing another fine Northwest Company schooner would be a major bonus to their war effort.

Meanwhile, British Lieutenant Colonel McDouall, commanding Mackinac Island, heard through the grapevine that the Americans were in his neighbourhood.

Bad timing for him!

Quite a number of men had left Mackinac for Prairie du Chien in response to a request for help there. He knew that it would only be a matter of time before the Americans attacked Mackinac. His only recourse was to get a message to John Johnston who, he knew, was at his home at the Sault.

Johnston assembled all able-bodied men in the area who then paddled like mad down the river, between the American mainland and Sugar Island.

Holmes and Turner, rowing their way to the Sault, missed seeing the canoes because they were making their way along Lake George, on the other side of that island.

A letter was later written, dated July 28, 1814, from Lieutenant Daniel Turner to Captain Arthur Sinclair, while aboard the *Scorpion* near Mackinac Island.[2]

Turner wrote that he "rowed night and day" in a launch to get to the Sault. Along the way, he shot an unspecified number of Natives, took other Natives as prisoners until he got to the Sault, while others avoided capture.

Burning the Sault

On July 23, 1814, at least one quick thinking, fast paddling Native got to the Sault, on the north side of the St. Marys River, beached his canoe, ran toward the Northwest Company holdings, located some Nor'westers, and emphatically explained that the Americans would be setting foot on their domain within the next two hours.

There was a major flurry of activity to get out of the Sault in the Perseverance, but the wind was not blowing in the right direction.

Time flew by too quickly, so that before anyone could catch his breath, about 150 Americans swarmed the Northwest's buildings, while Turner made his way into Lake Superior.

Captain Robert McCargo and the crew of the *Perseverance* had, just prior to Turner's unwelcome appearance, abandoned the schooner, hopped into a canoe and paddled furiously to get away, heading north along the eastern side of Lake Superior to Fort William.

In the area of Michipicoten, the group met up with Gabriel Franchère, and others, coming from Fort William. McCargo told Franchère that he had set fire to the heavily loaded schooner before escaping.

After arriving at Fort William and reporting to the Northwest Company, McCargo left to sail the only remaining Northwest Company schooner, the *Recovery* to Isle Royale, where he hid and camouflaged the ship in an inlet which is today called McCargo Cove.

Turner's letter to his superior, mentioned above, stated that the crew had set a few fires throughout their schooner, and "scuttled" her. Scuttle usually means that they tried to sink her by opening a valve in the hull, or creating a hole in the bottom, to let water in, or perhaps, in this case, scuttle just meant that the ship was to be sunk by a blazing fire.

Turner continued to write that he got on board the *Perseverance*, put out the fires, and "secured her from sinking." He did not explain how he managed this.

He then wrote that because the wind was not in his favour, he could not try to get the ship over the rapids until the 26th. [In his letter, to Croghan, Major Holmes stated the date as the 25th.] Turner described the rapids as follows: "The fall in three-quarters of a mile is forty-five feet and the channel very rocky, the current runs from twenty to thirty knots, and in one place there is a perpendicular leap of ten feet between three rocks."

At the three rocks, the *Perseverance* "bilged," was moving fast, and landed beneath the rapids, on the shore, where she became flooded with water.

Turner then had the *Perseverance* set on fire.

I suspect that Turner had no experience whatsoever with turbulent rapids!

He further explained that his plan had been to get the ship safely down the rapids and load her with the contents of the storehouses, but instead had to settle for four "captured boats" containing Native items.

The other items of value that were contained in four large buildings and two smaller ones were destroyed by fire. He noted that the goods had a value of between $50,000 and $100,000.

Fortunately, this was nowhere near the value of the furs expected to pass through the Sault sometime during the following month.

Normally food was stored at the Sault until it could be forwarded on to Fort William, but Turner did not specify what was contained in the buildings that belonged to the Northwest Company.

On the north side of the river - up in flames went all of the Northwest Company assets: their canal, canoe lock, and warehouses, although Turner only mentioned the warehouses in his letter.

Turner ended his letter by stating that "all private property was, according to your orders, respected."

This is in contrast to other reports that state that the huts of the fur traders were destroyed and we will later discover that private property was taken.

At the Sault, no one was around. Everyone available had gone to defend Mackinac.

Again, the Americans had a situation of no contest.

Holmes wrote to Lieutenant-Colonel Croghan, on July 27, 1814, from the *Scorpion*.[3] He stated that he had arrived at the Sault on the 23rd and that the Northwest Agent had already escaped with a "considerable amount of goods."

How he could have known what goods had disappeared in one canoe, I cannot predict.

He confirmed that the *Perseverance* had been set on fire by her crew, and later "bilged" when Turner tried to bring her over the rapids.

Further, Holmes wrote that "most of the goods . . . were found in the woods on the American side." He concluded that the goods were owned by John Johnston, who was not present, and who he considered a traitor.

He stated that [Johnston's] "agent armed the Indians from his stores at our approach, and, lastly, because those goods, or a considerable part, were designed to be taken to Michilimackinac. Pork, salt, and groceries...." - he seized them.

He did not write that he had Johnston's home and other property destroyed by fire but many other references do state that Johnston's assets were completely burned.

Johnston's wife, Ozhah-guscodaywayquay, with all but one of her children, escaped to safety, and the remaining child was not harmed.

Later, the Northwest Company received some compensation from the British government, but poor Johnston experienced exasperation in trying to obtain compensation.

His assets were on the south side of the St. Marys, clearly American territory, but he was fighting for the British.

No deals were made with him by either government.

Luckily for him, 13 years later, his wife and children received American land grants.

. . .

Meanwhile, Lieutenant-Colonel McDouall, on Mackinac Island, wrote to Lieutenant Miller Worsley, on July 28, advising that the Americans were in his vicinity, that he was expecting to be attacked any day, describing the huge fleet of ships and their guns, and advising Worsley to get his ship, the *Nancy*, as far up

Nottawasaga as he could and construct a log building, containing six pounders, to defend the *Nancy*. [4]

He knew that if the *Nancy* were captured, the people on Mackinac Island would starve during the following winter.

. . .

Captain Arthur Sinclair wrote his reporting letter to the U.S. Secretary of the Navy, from on board the *Niagara*, off of Mackinac Island, on July 29, 1814.[5] He stated that "the capture of the *Perseverence* [sic] gave us the complete command of Lake Superior."

I cannot determine what he was thinking when he wrote this statement. He did not explain how he was going to get a ship into Lake Superior. He did not appear to be aware that the Northwest Company had another ship on Lake Superior.

He lamented that he had been required to go to Mackinac Island, instead of going into Lake Superior, writing that had he been in Lake Superior, he could have taken over all assets situated on that lake, as well as Fort William. He felt that the fur trade would have been destroyed had he captured Fort William, given he believed that up to $2,000,000 worth of furs were at that fort at that time.

Further, he thought that severe damage had been done to Fort William, given the *Mink* and the *Perseverance*, with their loads of food supplies, would not be arriving, and he was convinced that those losses could not be replaced.

Assessing the Damage at the Sault

A group, comprised of Gabriel Franchère, Mr. D. Stuart, and two other men, arrived at the Northwest post at Batchewana, on July 29, and was told by some women there, who kindly did the cooking for them, that the post clerk, Frederick Goedike, had gone to the Sault to see what was happening there.

The following day, Goedike arrived back and described to them the situation at the Sault. In Franchère's journal, he wrote that Goedike had told him that 150 Americans had "sacked and pillaged everything that seemed to them of value belonging to the Northwest Company and to a Mr. Johnston."[6]

That same evening, William McGillivray arrived at Batchewana from Fort William.

The next day, everyone set out for the Sault to view the destruction of the Northwest Company assets.

Franchère wrote that "The sawmills, warehouses, houses and so forth had all been destroyed and were still smoking."[7] The schooner was at the foot of the rapids, completely burned.

Then, he and the others with him began creating a "defensive position" but he did not describe it.[8] Upon approach, some Natives, who were camped nearby, agreed to help if needed.

Meanwhile, as McGillivray's food supply had dwindled, his group was reduced to two meals per day.

McGillivray had sent an express canoe to Mackinac Island, on August 1, to let McDouall know what had transpired at the Sault; however, the messenger returned from Mackinac Island, on August 4, to advise that it had not been safe to approach that island because it was surrounded by American ships.

Franchère reported that McGillivray's group found Charles Ermatinger, "who had an attractive establishment. He had just finished building a windmill to encourage agriculture...."[9] Ermatinger showed them the wheat, growing there, that was three or four feet tall, as well as other grains.

Then, everyone went over to the south side of the river to view the damage there. Franchère wrote, regarding Nolin, "His house had an air of opulence and still bore traces of grandeur, which showed that he had formerly lived in considerable comfort."[10]

Franchère's next journal entry stated that they heard about the American attack on Mackinac Island.

By August 19, they were still at the Sault when two Northwest Company agents arrived from Fort William, in advance of canoes carrying a vast amount of fine furs.

Two days later, Franchère left for the mouth of the French River, with an advance group who were to check the route for Americans.

Fur Brigade

At some time around August 22, the Northwest Company's canoes arrived at Sault Ste. Marie, from Fort William, carrying furs worth not less than $1,000,000.

There was a lot of anxiety as to whether the Nor'westers could transport the furs to the mouth of the French River, without being attacked by the Americans.

The heavily armed men, numbering between 325 and 335, travelling in forty-four large canoes, arrived at the mouth of the French River during the evening of August 25th.

Luck was on their side.

No American ships were spotted along the way so that the furs were successfully transported into the French River, and then on to Montreal.

Re-enactment. of Battle of Mackinac Island 1814

www.mackinacparks.com/war-of-1812/

War 1812 by George S. May

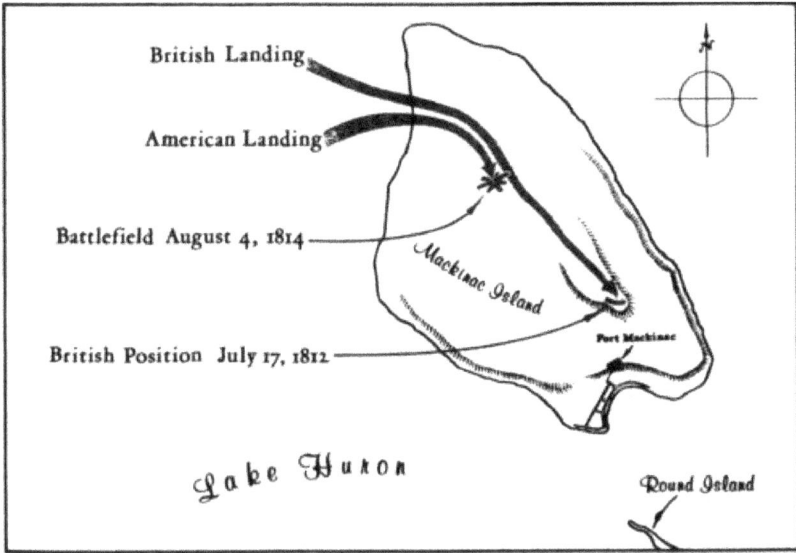

British Landing

American Landing

Battlefield August 4, 1814

British Position July 17, 1812

Mackinac Island

Fort Mackinac

Lake Huron

Round Island

Battle of Mackinac Island 1814

Lieutenant-Colonel George Croghan, who had a record of much success, commanded close to 1,000 men, specially chosen, for the land attack. Major Arthur Hunter Holmes, from Virginia, another excellent military man, was second to Croghan, as commander of the regular soldiers. Commodore Arthur Sinclair had in his command six large ships, along with launches and gunboats, with in excess of 500 sailors and marines on board.

The sailing weather had been less than ideal, but the American ships had been near Mackinac Island since July 26.

By August 4, it was about time to get on with it, but the Americans had not planned on attacking that day. They just wanted to check out the strength of their enemy.

**Attack on Mackinac.
Illustration by Peter Rindlisbacher**

Legion Canada's Military History Magazine,
August 1, 2013.

Meanwhile, McDouall was expecting the attack. The existing fort, situated on the south side of the island, was on a ridge overlooking the harbour.

Under his direction, another fort, named Fort George, now called Fort Holmes, was constructed on the top of the highest cliff. This gave him some comfort.

As to firepower, he had to count on the Natives to defend but was not overly confident that he should rely on them. Only time would tell if they would come through for him.[11]

Lieutenant-Colonel Croghan, on the advice of his guides, who had previously lived on the island, decided to try to land on the north-west of the island, where there was a break in the cliffs. His largest ships could anchor reasonably close to this shore, but the next step was not in his favour.

His men had to march almost two miles before arriving in an open area. The problem with the march was that it was through thick brush, shrubs, and trees.

McDouall wasted no time in moving forward, having his men hide in the thick underbrush along the edges of the open area, which incidentally, was Dousman's farm, and has been the Wawashkamo Golf Links since 1898.

The Americans could march straight ahead, or they could branch off on the paths that went around each flank, but McDouall simply did not have the manpower to protect the flanks.

As soon as the Americans were spotted, two of McDouall's field guns fired at them; however, no damage was done to the enemy.

The Americans responded to the field guns by

moving their regulars to their right flank.

Meanwhile, Holmes along with other officers were walking out in front, with Holmes casually swinging his sword, as if he did not have a care in the world.

A small band of Menominees, under Chief Tomah, stayed in position. Without missing a beat, Menominee L'Espagnol killed Major Holmes with the first shot. L'Espagnol was so named because he had some Spanish blood. His nephew, Yellow Dog, wounded the second-in-command, Captain Dresha, severely. They repeatedly fired from within the undergrowth until Captain Van Horne and Lieutenant Jackson were both fatally wounded.

With the loss of officers, the regulars entered a state of disarray.

Menominees In Position under Chief Tomah

Illustration by Dirk Gringhuis.
www.warof1812-bicentennial.info

The regulars then charged directly to the front but the Natives did not let up in firing at them from their hidden positions. The firing from the Natives was so accurate against the regulars that Croghan gave the order to retreat to their ships.

The battle was of a short duration but the loss of valuable men was incalculable.

The next morning, Croghan sent a flag to the battle area to check for wounded and to retrieve the body of Major Holmes.

His written report to the U.S. Secretary of War, dated August 9, 1814, indicated that fifty-seven of his men had been wounded and twenty-two had been killed.[12]

He then sent the militia and two regular companies to Detroit, along with Holmes' body and the wounded.

To reverse his defeat, he chose to take the other three companies to attack at Nottawasaga. If he could cut off the movement of food to Mackinac Island, he could starve it into surrender.

Captain Sinclair wrote to the U.S. Secretary of the Navy, from the *Niagara*, near Nottawasaga, on August 9. He explained that Mackinac had not been attacked sooner due to undesirable weather which prevented them from finding a prisoner who could tell them how strongly Mackinac was protected by the Natives.

There had been some encounters on a nearby island and based on those skirmishes, the Americans believed that a great many Natives were defending Mackinac.

They just did not know that the strength of the

Natives was greater than all of their combined forces.

In Sinclair's letter to the Secretary of the Navy, from the *Niagara*, on August 9, he stated:[14]

"Mackinac is by nature a perfect Gibraltar, being a high, inaccessible rock on every side except from the west, from which to the heights you have near two miles to pass through a wood so thick that our men were shot in every direction, and within a few yards of them, without being able to see the Indians who did it....the further our troops advanced the stronger the enemy became, and the weaker and more bewildered our force were; several of the commanding officers were picked out and killed or wounded without seeing any of them. The men were getting lost and falling into confusion . . . which demanded an immediate retreat or a total defeat..."

In fact, Mackinac Island was defended by about one hundred of the Royal Newfoundland Regiment and the Michigan Fencibles, comprised of about forty-five Canadian fur traders, along with the "gallant" Folles Avoines, and a "few" Winnibagoes, Chippewas, and Ottawas, for a total of 150 Natives.

Not a man was injured.

US Brig *Niagara*

https://archive.hnsa.org/ships/img/niagara1.jpg

General Robert McDouall (1774–1848)

Source: Dumfries and Galloway Council (Stranraer)
From Dictionary of Canadian Biography

Map – The Northern Theatre of War

War of 1812 Magazine Issue 4. Napoleon-series.org

THE NORTHERN THEATER

■ fort   ● battle site or town/village

Lake Superior

St. Joseph I.

Fort Mackinac

Lake Michigan

Lake Huron

Georgian Bay

Nottawasaga River

Nottawasaga Bay

L. Simcoe

MICHIGAN TERRITORY

St. Clair R.

York

Stoney Creek

Burlington Bay

Ft. George

Queenston

Fort N

Ft. Erie

Malcolm's Mills

Grand R.

Moraviantown

Thames R.

Port Dover

Long Point

Detroit

Detroit R.

Sandwich

Malden (Fort Amherstburg)

Raisin R.

Frenchtown

Port au Bois

Lake Erie

Erie

Fort Miami

Fort Meigs

ee River

Cleveland

PENNSYL

The people on Mackinac Island were at the point of starvation. McDouall had sent men out to buy food from the Natives but even they were near starvation.

Information had been obtained from a prisoner, taken from the *Mink*, that Mackinac Island was being supplied with food by loading it on to ships at the Nottawasaga River, in Georgian Bay.

From Mackinac Island, Sinclair and Croghan headed toward Georgian Bay with the *Tigress* and the *Scorpion*.

In addition to preventing food from getting to Mackinac, they wanted to attack boats, carrying furs, on their way from the Sault to the French River.

Collecting the value of the furs was a bonus, but the main objective was to defeat the fur traders by starvation.

The *Nancy* had been transporting provisions to Mackinac Island, and the threat that she would be captured by the Americans caused grave concern. In this regard, Lieutenant Miller Worsley, of the Royal Navy, along with a few seamen, reached the Nottawasaga River in mid-July, where he was to take over the schooner from Lieutenant Poyntz.

There they waited, for perhaps ten days, for the *Nancy's* return from Mackinac Island, while they endured terrible weather, and swatted mosquitoes.

As soon as the *Nancy* arrived, she was loaded with three hundred barrels of food provisions, as well as military items.

Meanwhile, Lieutenant Robert Livingston, (who had escaped from Hull soon after having been taken prisoner at Detroit) was on his way by canoe, with twenty-three Natives, to locate the *Nancy*, to deliver the letter written on July 28 by McDouall to Worsley.

They found the *Nancy* about two hours into her journey to Mackinac and upon receiving McDouall's letter, turned back to shore.

Immediately, the *Nancy* was taken as far as she could be towed up the Nottawasaga River, being a distance of two miles (about 3.34 km).

I cannot picture what towed the schooner. It may have been more a case of men dragging her along. The narrow river contained water that was six to eight feet in depth and was bordered with brush and rocks.

They managed to hide the *Nancy* so that she could not be spotted from Nottawasaga Bay. There were sand dunes, topped with some trees and bush, blocking her, in addition to a quickly constructed log blockhouse, containing three mounted guns. Two of them were twenty-four pounder carronades which had been removed from boats that were lying in the river. The remaining item was a six-pounder field piece.

Livingston, who had gone to York with dispatches, returned to the Nottawasaga River, during the morning of August 13, and went out to find Natives who could help defend the schooner, but was only able to gather together twenty-three of them.

During the early evening of August 13, the American schooners, *Scorpion* and *Tigress*, and the brig *Niagara*, all under the command of Lieutenant-Colonel Croghan arrived at the mouth of the Nottawasaga River.

The ships carried artillery, field guns, and three companies of regular infantry, being about three hundred men, all for the purpose of attacking one transport ship.

For the *Nancy's* protection, Worsley had Midshipman Dobson, twenty-three Royal Navy seamen, nine French Canadian boatmen, and Livingston with his twenty-three Natives, for a total of fifty-seven men.

Worsley's men had placed a line of powder from the blockhouse to the *Nancy*. If a shot were fired into the blockhouse, the nearby combustible material would ignite, which would then blow up, causing a ferocious fire to race toward the *Nancy* to consume her, with her cargo, within minutes.

Croghan went out during the evening of his arrival to look around for a spot to encamp. While walking, he just happened to notice the *Nancy*.

The following morning, Sinclair fired from his ships but had no result because the sand dunes and trees prevented clear vision.

At about noon, two howitzers were taken to shore and set up.

This time, the effect was so overwhelming that Worsley made the decision to fire into the blockhouse to destroy the *Nancy* and its load of food supplies. He and his men then ran for the bush.[14]

HMS Nancy

Later, Croghan claimed in his reporting letter of the incident, that one of his shells caused the explosion.[15]

In any event, the *Nancy* was completely destroyed.

Sinclair's written report stated that he did not know if the men defending the *Nancy* had been blown up in the blockhouse or whether they had escaped to their rear, downhill into a thickly wooded area.[16]

Croghan and Sinclair were satisfied that

Mackinac Island would starve, given no other ships were on Lake Huron to transport food

Before departing on aboard the Niagara, Sinclair chose twenty-five men from the infantry to serve as marines on the two ships to be left at the Nottawasaga River, being the *Tigress* and the *Scorpion*, and provided the *Scorpion* with a boarding netting to protect against a night attack by small boats.

On August 15, Sinclair left for Lake Erie, leaving Lieutenant Turner as commander of the *Scorpion* and the *Tigress*, with strict instructions to deny any canoe or boat entry to, or exit from, the Nottawasaga River.

The Americans cut down trees and blocked the river to ensure that no one could get in or out without their knowledge.

They did not stick around though because one of their men was wounded by one of the Natives who continued to fire at the Americans.

Sinclair had also directed that the *Tigress* could be sent to cruise around St. Joseph Island for one or two weeks at a time to intercept canoes carrying furs toward the French River

Unbeknown to the Americans, about one hundred barrels of supplies, destined for Mackinac Island, were in a storehouse further up the Nottawasaga River. As two batteaux, as well as Livingston's large canoe, were still available, these were loaded with seventy barrels of supplies.

On the night of August 18, the trees were quietly removed from the mouth of the river, and Livingston, with Worsley and crew, got away, unnoticed by anyone.

Map Nottawasaga River

View of Nottawasaga River,
flowing from Georgian Bay,
at Wasaga Beach, Ontario.

Marinas.com

Flour to the Rescue

Sometime during August, the Americans were tipped off about a Canadian food supply brigade making its way down the French River toward Lake Huron.

To intercept it, the *Scorpion* was sent out for five days, sailing between St. Joseph Island and the French River.

Meanwhile, Captain J.M. LaMothe was commanding that brigade of government canoes, carrying the valuable provisions, from Montreal to Mackinac Island.

Before the brigade reached Lake Huron, it received word that the Americans were on the lake.

There was almost a mutiny.

The crew had no desire whatsoever to be captured or they refused to proceed into the lake.

I do not know how messages were dispatched so fast, but they were!

Deputy Assistant Commissary General George Crookshank was in York [now Toronto] but he managed to keep three of the canoes moving by bribing the crew.

LaMothe returned to Montreal to get other canoes and crews, but Crookshank did not feel certain that he would return with more provisions. Crookshank consulted with Lieutenant-Colonel Drummond regarding the problem and was directed to ask "steady" Natives to take charge of the eleven remaining canoes.[17]

Drummond's next step was to direct as many batteaux as necessary to be taken from York to

Nottawasaga River to transport food across Lake Huron.

Simultaneously, Crookshank put plans into action for men to take canoe loads of flour, in particular, by following the coastline to a depot at the Sauganock River. From there, the supplies would be moved to the Thessalon River, from which provisions could be moved over the ice during winter to Mackinac Island.

Three batteaux were arranged to make two trips, with flour, to the depot.

Soon after, he planned on having enough manpower and canoes to make up the six hundred barrels that were required to keep the folks on Mackinac Island fed during the coming winter.

Ships, or no ships, Mackinac Island was not going to starve!

Trouble on the Horizon

Some Natives had set out from Mackinac for the Sault and got as far as St. Joseph Island when they turned around and went back to Mackinac Island. Their reason for making a hasty return was to report to McDouall that, on August 25, they saw American ships sailing around St. Joseph Island.

Lieutenant Worsley wrote a report letter, dated September 15, 1814, to Sir James L. Yeo, wherein he outlined his activities since leaving Nottawasaga.[18]

He explained that he and his crew left Nottawasaga on August 18, carrying flour in two batteaux, and after six days of travelling, safely arrived to "within eight miles of St. Joseph Island."

That same day, being August 24, he spotted two American schooners, sailing "between the islands opposite St. Joseph's." He could not pass them because the channel was too narrow. Therefore, he decided to safely hide the batteaux containing the flour.

In this regard, Livingston, whose home had been on St. Joseph Island, prior to the commencement of the war, was able to choose the best location. The two batteaux were pulled up and hidden, but he did not explain exactly where.

The men then set out in a canoe, travelling through the night toward Mackinac Island. During the night of August 29, they managed to quietly paddle pass the American ships, without being noticed. The next day, they landed on Mackinac Island, at sunset.

Immediately, Worsley asked McDouall for

permission to return to attack the two American Schooners.

McDouall knew that it would be risky. If Worsley's men were spotted, all of them could be killed.

Worsley was confident that he could pull it off.

McDouall granted permission on the condition that, as a safety measure, a chosen group of Native warriors would accompany them. Dickson, who was always at the right place at the right time, stepped up and volunteered to lead the warriors although he had plenty of help from Assiginack.

On that note, four boats were made ready.

Revenge by Batteaux

On September 1, the revengers set out from Mackinac Island, travelling 36 miles [60 km] to De Tour by the next night.

Lieutenant Bulger, with a three-pounder, commanded a detachment of the Royal Newfoundland Regiment, while Worsley commanded his seamen, in his batteau, carrying a six-pounder. Each of Lieutenants Armstrong and Radenhurst commanded the other two batteaux.

Livingston was also part of the group of fifty men, plus Dickson and the Natives.

Odawa Chief Assiginack, of Manitoulin Island, led the Natives, who held back in the rear, about three miles.

Worsley later wrote that he felt "great obligation to Mr. Dickson....for the good order and regularity they observed the whole time."[20]

It may have been that Chief Assiginack had influence in this as well.

The following morning, being September 3, their boats were hidden in a bay while Worsley went out in a canoe to observe the American boats' positions.

He noticed one of the schooners, at anchor, about six miles away, in the middle of the De Tour channel.

He returned to his men, and they waited until 6:00 p.m. before setting out.

By 9:00 p.m., they were within thirty feet (9.144 meters) of the schooner.

At this point, the schooner hailed them.

They did not respond.

The schooner fired on them but missed.

The American sailors fired small arms at them.

In the midst of the firing, the attackers kept moving quietly, but with lightning speed.

Worsley and Armstrong approached on the starboard side and the boats of Bulger and Radenhurst attacked on the harbourside.

They were beside the schooner and onto its deck, all within five minutes, and into a quick hand-to-hand battle.

The Americans retreated below deck but fired muskets up which resulted in one of Worsley's seamen being killed.

It was the *Tigress*.

The American ship carried a long twenty-four-pounder, and officers and men numbering thirty-one.

The American commander, Sailing Master Champlin, was severely wounded, as were his officers. His losses were four wounded, one killed, and three missing who, Worsley was advised, had been killed and thrown overboard.

On Worsley's side, two seamen were killed, while Bulger and seven soldiers received minor wounds.

Early the next morning, the prisoners were taken, under guard, in batteaux, to Mackinac Island.

The retaliation was now fifty percent completed!

Scorpion Attack

Without delay, on September 4th, Worsley got ready to attack the only remaining American ship on the upper Great Lakes. He believed that the ship was at anchor, somewhere among the islands, but not very close by.

Livingston was sent out in his canoe as a scout. Within two hours he was back to advise that the ship was heading their way.

Worsley felt that there was no way that the approaching ship could have heard the firing, while the first ship was being captured, and so was very confident that the second ship had no knowledge whatsoever as to the fate of the *Tigress*. Therefore, he kept the American flag flying.

When the ship caught up to within two miles of the *Tigress*, she dropped anchor for the night.

Meanwhile, some of Worsley's men had hidden themselves away in the hold or the cabin. Other soldiers were on the deck but had changed into American uniforms.

During the night, possibly close to dawn, Worsley gave the order to weigh anchor. They then sailed toward the other ship under their jib and foresail. He wrote that he kept ten or twelve men on deck. As he approached, he could see that the other ship suspected nothing, given they were washing their decks.

At about thirty-six feet (eleven meters) from the ship, Worsley fired a long twenty-four-pounder. This action indicated to his soldiers to get up on deck and start firing.

The USS Tigress alongside the USS Scorpion

Legionmagazine.com

Worsley, himself, wasted not a second in going over the side of the enemy boat, while his soldiers fired. He was promptly followed by his seamen, and thereafter came the soldiers.

Worsley's reporting letter stated: "She was immediately carried," and the British flag was hoisted on the *Scorpion*.

No fooling around!

The *Scorpion* had been commanded by Turner, and carried five officers and thirty-one seamen, with one long twenty-four-pounder and one long twelve-pounder. The loss to the Americans was two killed and two wounded.

On Worsley's side, only one was wounded.

Some privately-owned items that had been plundered from residents at the Sault and St. Joseph Island were discovered on the ship.

The celebratory cheers must have been deafening as the two confiscated ships were sailed back to Mackinac Island.

Regarding Worsley, McDouall wrote to Drummond, on September 9th, 1814, stating: "his active and indefatigable mind never rested till he had relieved us from such troublesome neighbours and conducted the blocking force in triumph into our port." [19]

Worsley gave both ships new names. The *Tigress* became the *Confiance* and the *Scorpion* became the *Surprise*.

Both ships immediately returned to Nottawasaga, picked up six months' worth of provisions, and reached Mackinac Island in early October.

The fur traders no longer had fear of the Americans confiscating their cargoes or trying to starve them into submission, and Mackinac Island was held securely in British hands until the end of the war.

Treaty of Ghent

The Treaty of Ghent[20] was signed on Christmas Eve of 1814, ending the war. It specified that all captured lands would revert to their original owners.

Then, the operative words of the treaty were, "restoring upon principles of perfect reciprocity, Peace, Friendship, and good Understanding between them...."

This clause has held firm for 200 years among the British, Canadians, and Americans.

The ninth Article of the treaty stated that the Americans, Canadians, and Natives would stop fighting with each other and that Canada and the United States would "restore to such Tribes or Nations respectively all the possessions, rights, and privileges, which they may have enjoyed or been entitled to in one thousand eight hundred and eleven previous to such hostilities."

This restoration did not effectively happen.

Interestingly, the matter of slavery was included in the treaty. The tenth article of the treaty stated: "Whereas the Traffic in Slaves is irreconcilable with the principles of humanity and Justice, and whereas both His Majesty and the United States are desirous of continuing their efforts to promote its entire abolition, it is hereby agreed that both the contracting parties shall use their best endeavours to accomplish so desirable an object."

The matter of slavery was not addressed in the United States until its civil war.

Effects of the Treaty of Ghent

The British garrison, along with many Canadians, vacated Mackinac in 1815 to take up residence on Drummond Island, instead of the run-down military post at St. Joseph Island.

Historically, a sad incident happened when vacating Mackinac in that all of the official documents from 1796 to 1814 for Fort St. Joseph were lost and never located.

With the move to Drummond Island came the problem of arranging for housing. Materials were not available, nor was there skilled labour. Therefore, some buildings on St. Joseph Island were repaired and moved over to Drummond Island.

The Fort St. Joseph bakehouse was used as a barrack for about eight military men who guarded the magazine from 1815 to 1828.

Between 1818 and 1835, there are no records as to activity on St. Joseph Island, although there may have been Natives living there, at least seasonally to make maple sugar.

Samuel Peck was on the Island by 1839, or sooner, where he operated a store at Gosh-ka-Wong (aka Milford Haven).

In 1844, Peck married Josephte Rocbert de la Morandière on the Island and also made out his Will there. It was witnessed by Jean Baptiste Rousseau, James Prior who was Josephte's eldest son, and thirdly by Frederic Lamorandière, Josephte's brother.

Étienne Rocbert de la Morandière and Sai Sai Go No Kwe, who had been living at Killarney since 1820, retired to St. Joe Island, in 1845, for some time.

In 1822, The International Boundary Commission placed Drummond Island in the United States.

It was decided that establishing a new garrison in the north, at Sault Ste. Marie, Pointe aux Pins, or St. Joseph Island, would be too expensive to maintain, so the garrison would be moved to Penetanguishene.

When Drummond Island was turned over to the Americans on November 14, 1928, the garrison, with about seventy-five Canadian families, moved to Penetanguishene aboard the Wellington and the Alice Hackett.

There, land grants were conveyed in recognition of the homes that had been abandoned. Some of the people were French and others were Métis, such as Charles Langlade, Jr, son of Capt. Langlade, who had grown up on Mackinac Island and then moved to St. Joseph Island.

All had been involved with the fur trade and had participated in the war.

Some later moved back to St. Joseph Island and the Sault.

The Upshot

Jefferson had failed to realize that there was goodwill between the British crown and the Native Indians.

In addition, Tecumseh, who had been fighting the Americans regarding land they had taken from the Natives, gladly joined the British, becoming an important leader in the defence of Canada.

The War of 1812 - 1814 began by a declaration of war on Great Britain by the United States of America because Britain had seized four hundred American ships in the course of enforcing its blockade against France during its war with Napoleon Bonaparte.

On the Atlantic Ocean, the United States had six ships taking shots at about one thousand ships of the British Navy. Early in the war, the U.S. did knock out some of the British ships, but my guess is that if there are one thousand items to aim at, then a few of them could be hit.

Aside from this slight ocean success, the blockade by the British eventually caused huge financial difficulties for the U.S.A.

The dispute had nothing to do with Canada, but there was no way that the U.S. was strong enough to attack Britain on its soil, so the U.S. went with its next best idea which was to hit Canada, with a view to taking it from Britain.

Canada, or any country, could not be conquered until the invader's boots were firmly on the ground, and in that regard, the Americans focused on Upper Canada, now Ontario.

Had we lost, we would now be American, but their

boots were only fleetingly on our soil.

For the United States, it may have been a continuation of its revolution, in that it was flexing its wings of independence.

The British agreed to end the shipping confrontation before the war began but this communication did not reach Washington until after the war was declared.

Instead of stopping the war, the Americans allowed it to continue.

Perhaps the American motivation to keep fighting was in accordance with its policy of *manifest destiny* which was the American belief that God had given them their country and that it should occupy all of North America.

Our Canadian ancestors disagreed.

As with most wars, the result should have come about without fighting.

Following the war, came peace and trade between Britain and Canada with the United States of America.

Many of the people who had to involve themselves in the war were friends and relatives. About sixty percent of the people living in Canada had moved here from the U.S.A. during the American Revolution because they were "true blue" to the English crown.

The other forty percent had come from various countries including France, England, Scotland, and Ireland.

All of them just wanted to live quietly and progress. They really had no desire to fight with anyone about anything. Disputes among themselves were settled diplomatically, not by firing a gun.

Until this war erupted, the border between the two countries was ignored because there was no reason to focus on it. However, once the shooting began, the inhabitants of Canada fiercely defended their borders and took the offence regarding American lands.

The waterways between the U.S.A. and Canada were the means of transportation and communication; however, those rivers and lakes were dominated by British ships and Canadian canoes.

Communication by Canadians was conducted by means of men in express canoes carrying letters to their destination.

The American means of delivering mail was conveyed on horseback. So, it happened that the war was on for a month before many American commanders knew about it.

The Americans declared war on Britain, but the land battles were fought against the people of Canada, who won this war through ingenuity and a huge amount of help from our unsung Natives.

Given the brilliant accomplishments in defending our borders, this war was no draw.

By the end of the war, we were no longer Natives, Fur Traders, French, English, and Settlers. We were Canadian!

Our next step was Confederation.

The people from St. Joseph Island, the Sault, and vast surrounding areas, although content with their accomplishment, had no idea at the time, how important their quick and determined action was to Canada.

The significance of the remains of old Fort St. Joseph is that it is a reminder to us that our ancestors made a major contribution to keeping Canada for the Canadians and that they achieved their objective in an extremely honourable manner, without firing a shot.

Where Did the Defenders Go?

Captain Charles Roberts took it upon himself to organize a company of fur traders for the protection of Mackinac Island in early 1813, which company was called the Michigan Fencibles that later saw action at Prairie du Chien.

In May, 1813, due to his deteriorating health condition, Roberts requested leave.

He left Mackinac Island in September, 1813 and endured a strenuous trip to Montreal.

With no possibility of a cure for his health problems, he requested retirement, but with bureaucracy being then as complicated as it is now, his request was not quickly addressed.

In 1815, he returned to England, where there was nothing further that could be done for his health, and he died a year later, at age 44 years.

It has been reported that he was an uncle to Field Marshall Roberts who was one of the most successful British commanders of the 19th century, who became the 1st Earl Roberts in recognition of his achievements.

General William Hull was sent to Quebec as a prisoner of war upon his surrender of Detroit and his troops in Michigan Territory. Once he was released he endured a trial and was court-martialed. Although his sentence was death, it was commuted.

He died a natural death in 1825, reconfirming that surrendering Detroit was the right decision to avoid much bloodshed.

Lieutenant Porter Hanks, as we know, died at Detroit during the day that it was surrendered to Brock.

Lieutenant Miller Worsley became ill in October, 1814 with Lake Fever which had symptoms similar to Yellow Fever. Many sailors on the Great Lakes had become ill with Lake Fever during the war.

In July, 1815, Worsley was appointed Commander, on half-pay, but did not take part in any further active service.

Post-war, he returned to the Isle of Wight, where he married in 1820.

He became Inspecting Commander in the Coast Guard and stayed at that post from 1832 – 1834, after which he retired.

The following year, he died, at age 43, and was survived by his wife and three children.

John Askin, Jr. had family connections with many Natives in the areas of Mackinac Island, St. Joseph Island, and Sault Ste. Marie so that it was natural for him to act as an interpreter for them.

He was most unhappy that the British government allowed Mackinac Island to be returned to the Americans as part of the peace treaty.

Not much was written about him following the war of 1812 – 1814.

He died on January 1, 1820 at approximately age 58 – 61 years.

Robert Ramsay Livingston had been retired from the Royal Navy sometime prior to the start of the war.

He had served four years as a midshipman on the Argus and eight years as an ensign in the 2nd Battalion, Royal Canadian Volunteers.

He then became a fur trader and was living comfortably on St. Joseph Island when the war began. There, he raised a group of thirty-six volunteers that he led to the attack on Mackinac.

As a fur trader, according to McDouall, Livingston had a reputation of being "a kind of smuggler between St. Joseph and Mackinac." I could not determine his exact smuggling acts.

By 1813, he was appointed to the position of Captain in the Indian Department of Upper Canada. In this capacity, the Natives referred to him as Miskinankai (the Fox).

According to Bayliss, his house, store, and wharf at St. Joe were burned by the Americans in 1814.

During the war, he was wounded a few times during battles at other places.

The information that I located about him post-war was unflattering. He petitioned for advancement in the Indian Department; however, McDouall was against Livingston having a position that involved responsibility due to his reputation as having harmful, hostile habits.

McDouall stated in a letter, dated February 25, 1816, to Secretary Foster that when Livingston arrived at Detroit with prisoners of war that had been captured at Mackinac Island, in 1812, he was not taken as a prisoner of war. Instead, he was thrown in jail because he owed £2,000 on account of unpaid trade goods.

McDouall further wrote: "other matters *still more strange* are stated of him about this period . . ."

Livingston formally claimed that he was the leader in capturing the *Tigress* and the *Scorpion*. McDouall disagreed and wrote: "As for his piloting the boats to the attack of the Enemy's Schooners: every body [sic] knew their precise station." His inference was that no leadership was required.

Robert Dickson continued, throughout the war, to gather together Natives to fight for the British, and determine where they could best be used, and he did it well.

During the summer of 1813, he brought about 1,400 Natives to Fort Malden [Amherstburg, Ontario] for its defence.

He took part in various battles over a vast area and was at Mackinac Island for its defence in 1814.

In 1815 or 1816, he became Lieutenant-Colonel and retired from the Indian Department with a pension.

His efforts had been vital to defending Canada; however, the war ruined his fur trade business.

In 1818, he began to work as an agent for Astor's American Fur Company in the Mississippi area and continued at this endeavour until he died suddenly on Drummond Island on June 20, 1823, at about age 57.

Jean Baptiste Toussaint Pothier lived a wealthy lifestyle in Montreal.

St. Joseph Island was never noted as his permanent residence, but he was often there on business and I believe that he kept a house there for himself for many years.

He was a member of the Legislative Council of Lower Canada from 1824 to 1838.

Then, he had a hand in approving the union of Upper and Lower Canada.

At the age of 49, he married, for the first time, an under-aged girl with whom he had a daughter. He died at the age of 74 years.

William McKay took an active part in the war throughout. In early 1814, he took command of the Michigan Fencibles.

After the Treaty of Ghent, it was his duty to advise the Natives to create good relations with the Americans. He met with them, various times, on Drummond Island during 1817 and 1818 to explain Britain's new policy regarding Natives. This was the start of the Indian Reserve system. As Superintendent of Indian Affairs at Drummond Island, from 1810 to 1828, he was required to implement this program. The Canadian government, instead of honouring and respecting the Natives who so gallantly came to the rescue of Upper and Lower Canada, made them wards.

McKay moved to Montreal where he was the Superintendent of the Indian Department for the area of Montreal beginning in 1830.

He died at the age of 60 years of cholera, during its epidemic in that city in 1832.

John Johnston had been born into the gentry of Northern Ireland and was known to all who knew him as a perfect gentleman.

He had never been able to accept the way the Northwest Company and Hudson's Bay Company conducted business.

In 1811, he was planning on moving to the Montreal area to take up life as a gentleman farmer, but the war got in the way and it cost him dearly.

He died on September 22, 1828, at Sault, Michigan, at the age of 66, and was granted a military burial.

Charles Oakes Ermatinger retired with his family to a farm at Longue-Pointe in the Montreal area, in 1827.

Although he and Charlotte already had thirteen children of which eight had survived infancy, on September 6, 1832, they were married in Christ Church in Montreal.

Ermatinger died on September 4, 1833, at the age of 57 years.

Chief Shingwaukonce of Garden River
(1773 – 1854)
Dick Pine Fonds,
Shingwauk Residential School Centre

Chief Shingwauk fought in the Battle of Mackinac Island, and also fought in other battles of this war in southern Ontario, as did many other Indigenous, including Tecumseh.

The Algoma Board of Education produced the video, *The Anishinaabe View – In Their Own Words,* wherein the current chief of Batchewana, Dean Sayers, stated that Shingwauk had fought beside General Issac Brock, who just before he was killed, gave his sword to Shingwauk. Sometime much later, the building at Garden River, where the sword was kept, burned completely. Right after this fire, the sword went missing.

I understand from Sayers that Shingwauk also had been given the epaulettes from Brock's uniform.

Post-war, I believe Shingwauk was awarded at least three medals and those may still be in the hands of the Pine family.

Sayers also advised in that Batchewana Chief Wabechechake was killed at the Battle of Fort George, in the Niagara Falls area.

Chief Shingwauk was originally from south of Lake Superior; however, in 1836, he helped establish Garden River [Kitigaun Seebee] where many of his descendants still reside.

Shingwaukonse died in 1854 at the age of 81 years.

At some point, quite a number of Métis from the Sault moved to Garden River after having been pushed out by non-native settlers.

The Cadotte family had been in the Sault area since 1671 and during the late 1800s married into the Pine family.

I believe other Métis families, such as Biron, Belleau, Corbiere, and Boissoneau, among others, also married into Garden River families.

Jean Baptiste Nolin bought the trading post at Michipicoten from Alexander Henry in 1777.

He moved to Mackinac Island in 1781 and travelled back and forth between Mackinac and the Sault until the late 1780s when he settled in the Sault. Thereafter, he and Johnston were the centres of influence and activity at the Sault.

Nolin was convinced to move to the Selkirk

colony, at Pembina, North Dakota in 1819 at which time he sold his interests at the Sault to Ermatinger.

Nolin died in 1826 at the age of 84 years.

Michael Dousman reconfirmed his allegiance to the U.S.A. after the war but was not permitted to have further business dealings with the Canadians.

He went on to become very wealthy.

In addition, to the fur trade, he developed other business interests such as the Straits of Mackinac water-powered sawmill. I believe this has been reconstructed in the Historic Mill Creek State Park.

He lived to be 83 years of age.

Lieutenant-Colonel Robert McDouall was devastated when Mackinac Island was returned to the Americans.

He oversaw the handover of Mackinac Island on July 18, 1815, and then commanded at Drummond Island until June, 1816, when he returned to Stranraer, Scotland, where he spent the balance of his life.

Before leaving Drummond Island, he arranged for William McKay to sit for a portrait. I gather there may have been others who sat for portraits which McDouall wanted to have on his walls at his home in Scotland.

In 1817, he was appointed as a Companion of the Order of the Bath in recognition of his accomplishments at Mackinac Island.

Although he was never again called to take part in active service, he was promoted to Colonel in 1830 and to Major-General in 1841.

McDouall never married and spent considerable time and money on the Free Church of Scotland.

He died at age 73.

Charles Langlade, Jr. moved to Drummond Island and then relocated to Penetanguishene with his family. His daughter, Marguerite, later became the second wife of George Gordon.

Étienne Rocbert de la Morandière and Sai-sai-go-no-kwe lived on Drummond Island post-war, where they operated a provisions and dry goods store. Unfortunately, their property was destroyed by fire in 1817. They would have been completely ruined except that they had goods at Flat Point, (White Fish Bay) North Channel of Lake Huron.

They then lived and traded at Flat Point, until June of 1820 when they established a fur trading post at Killarney, Ontario.

In 1845, they went to live on St. Joseph Island for a while with their son, Charles, and at some point, returned to Killarney.

Sai-sai-go-no-kwe's parents were Ottawa and Shawnee. Through her mother, she was a close relative of Tecumseh – a cousin, I believe.

Étienne lived to be 92 while Sai-sai-go-no-kwe reached 88 years.

George Gordon moved from Drummond Island to Penetanguishene in 1825 and is credited with being the founder of the town.

He was the son of Lady Jane Cook and Lieutenant Gabriel Gordon of the 60th Regiment.

Jane was my great-great-great-great grandmother by her relationship with Dominique Rousseau [now there's a story] which produced five sons, three of whom became clerks in the fur trade.

Charles Rousseau married Jessie Solomon, of Mackinac Island, who was of German Jewish and Native background.

They moved from Drummond Island to Penetanguishene for a brief period of time and then returned to St. Joseph Island.

Their daughter, Angelique, married Tudor Rains, and they moved to Sault, Michigan, where there are still descendants of theirs residing.

Jean Baptiste Rousseau married Julie, daughter of Étienne and Sai-sai-go-no-kwe, at Drummond Island in 1825, in a lavish wedding ceremony. They moved to Penetanguishene for some time and then moved back to St. Joseph Island.

He died suddenly in 1867 after having been the returning officer at Bruce Mines for the first election and is buried at Gosh-ka-wong, St. Joseph Island.

Julie then moved to Sault, Michigan, to live with her daughter, Charlotte LaLonde.

Julie, as we know had been on Mackinac Island when it fell to the British/Canadians. She died four days past her 100th birthday.

About the Author

Sandra Rousseau combined her skills of researching, interviewing, writing, and editing to create a career as an author, after working for 35 years in law, both in Canada and the U.S.

A Millennium was the result of her extensive research extending back into the 8th century which follows a family of Vikings attacking Normandy, followed by England in 1066 with William the Conqueror, and in the 12th century relocating to Scotland, then to Northern Ireland in the 17th century, followed by North America in the mid-19th century.

Children of the Fallen Snow was her next research project which delved into her French and Indigenous paternal ancestry. Research discovered her ancestral familial connection with Tecumseh, as well as Ottawa Chief Me-sa-sa, both of whom fought against the settlers' expansion in Ohio. The Battle of Fallen Timbers, on August 20, 1794, is considered to have been the last battle of the American Revolution. Me-sa-sa's life ended, as he stood on what became known as Turkey Foot Rock, while rallying his warriors, when General Anthony Wayne's army shot him off the rock. Tecumseh went on to fight in Canada in the War of 1812 – 1814 and was ultimately killed in the Battle of the Thames River. Then, through in-depth research and testing of various people, Sandra uncovered her Indigenous DNA, which goes back thousands of years in North America.

Her most recent book is entitled *Sault Ste. Marie and Beyond*. This is history, as it happened, on both sides of the turbulent rapids at the Sault, dividing a settlement into two countries. In the Upper Peninsula of Michigan and southern Lake Superior, historical characters tell their stories in their own words: the Anishinaabe defeating the destructive Iroquois; the travels and determination of the Jesuit priests; Alexander Henry's adventures from Mackinac Island to Lake Superior; fur traders with Indigenous wives evolving into a new culture. The book explores the culture of the Anishinaabe homeland; French fur trade commerce; entrepreneurs' shipbuilding and copper mining; war declared by the Americans; Canada rescued by its Indigenous neighbours; and religious encroachment. Ultimately, creating a vibrant Sault Ste. Marie.

Ermatinger-Clergue National Historic Site

At Ermatinger-Clergue National Historic Site,
Bay Street, Sault Ste. Marie, Ontario.
Left to Right: Curator: Kathryn Fisher,
Author: Sandra Rousseau, Will Hollingshead.
Photo by Corey Marques, April, 2018.

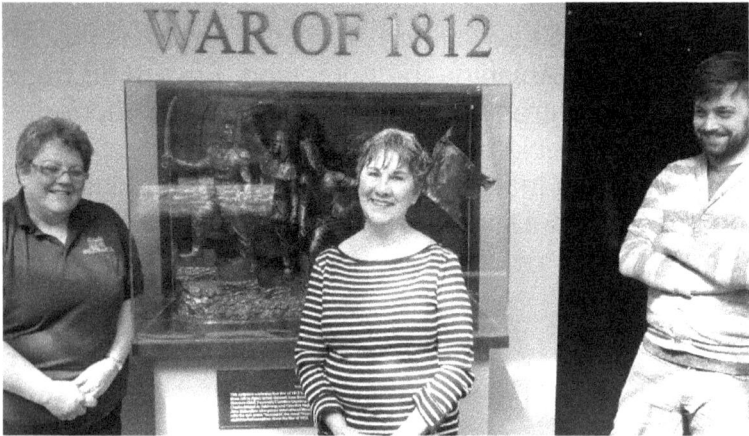

Endnotes

1. The quote is contained in Lieut.-Col. E. Cruikshank's An Episode of the War of 1812. The Story of the Schooner "Nancy," contained in Papers and Records of the Ontario Historical Society, Vol. 9, page 97.
2. Cruikshank page 98 - 99.
3. Cruikshank page 99 – 100.
4. From Niles' Register, Vol. VII, page 132. Captured by Capt. Sinclair at Nottawasaga. Cruikshank page 100 - 101.
5. Cruikshank page 99.
6. The quote is contained in Gabriel Franchère's Journal, page 184.
7. Franchère page 184.
8. Franchère page 184.
9. Franchère page 185.
10. Franchère page 185.
11. Cruikshank pages 107 - 108.
12. Cruikshank pages 103 -105.
13. Cruikshank page 101.
14. Canadian Archives, Series C, Vol. 685, page 145 and Cruikshank pages 111 – 112: George Crookshank's letter to Peter Turquand, Deputy Commissary General, dated August 21, 1814.
15. Cruikshank pages 112 – 113: Croghan's letter to Brig.-Gen. Duncan McArthur, dated August 23, 1814.
16. Cruikshank pages 113 – 114: Sinclair's letter to the Secretary of the Navy, dated September 3,

1814.

17.   Canadian Archives, Series C. Vol. 685, page 168 and Cruikshank pages 116 – 117: Lieut.-Gen. Drummond's letter to Prevost, dated September 5, 1814.

18.   Canadian Archives, Series M. Volume 6, page 202 and Cruikshank pages 120 – 123.

19.   Canadian Archives, Series C, Vol. 685, page 176 and Cruikshank pages 119 – 120.

20.   Hunter.

Bibliography

Abbott, John, Graeme S. Mount, Michael J. Mulloy. *The History of Fort St. Joseph*. Toronto: Dundurn, 2000.

Allen, Robert S. "WILLIAM McKAY," in Dictionary of Canadian Biography, vol 6, University of Toronto/Université Laval, 2003-, accessed May 3, 2018, http://www.biographi.ca/en/McKay_William_6E.html.

Armour, David A. "JOHNSTON, JOHN," in *Dictionary of Canadian Biography*, vol. 6, University of Toronto/Université Laval, 2003–, accessed May 3, 2018, http://www.biographi.ca/en/bio/johnston_john_6E.html

Askin, John. *The John Askin Papers.* Vol. 2. Ed. Milo Milton Quaife. Burton Historical Records, Detroit. Detroit Library Commission. 1928 – 1931.

Bayliss, Joseph, Estelle Bayliss. *Historic St. Joseph Island.* Cedar Rapids, Iowa: Torch, 1938.

Berton, Pierre. *The Capture of Detroit.* Toronto: McClelland & Stewart, 1991.

Chaput, Donald, "NOLIN, JEAN-BAPTISTE (d. 1826)," in *Dictionary of Canadian Biography*, vol. 6, University of Toronto/Université Laval, 2003–, accessed May 3, 2018, http://www.biographi.ca/en/bio/nolin_jean_baptiste_18 26_6E.html.

Chute, Janet E. *The Legacy of Shingwaukonse, A Century of Native Leadership*. University of Toronto Press Incorporated, 1998.

Cruikshank, Lieut.-Col. E. (1853 – 1939). *An Episode of the War of 1812. The Story of the Schooner "Nancy"* in Papers and Records of the Ontario Historical Society, Vol. 9, 1910.

Franchère, Gabriel (1786 – 1863). *Journal of a voyage on the north west coast of North America during the years 1811, 1812, 1813, 1814.* Ed. William Kaye Lamb. Champlain Society, 45. Toronto: 1969.

Friesen, Gerald "FRANCHÈRE, GABRIEL," in *Dictionary of Canadian Biography*, vol. 9, University of Toronto/Université Laval, 2003–, accessed May 3, 2018, http://www.biographi.ca/en/bio/franchere_gabriel_9E. html.

Hunter, Miller, Ed. *Treaties and Other International Acts of the United States of America*, Vol. 2. Washington: Government Printing Office, 1931.

May, George S. *War 1812*.Mackinac Island State Park Commission 1962.

Morrison, Jean. *Superior Rendezvous Place Fort William in the Canadian Fur Trade*. Toronto. Natural Heritage/Natural History. 2001.

Newman, Peter C. *Caesars of the Wilderness*. New York. Penguin, 1987.

Osborne, A. C. *The Migration of Voyageurs from Drummond Island to Penetanguishene in 1828*. Ontario Historical Society Papers and Records, Vol. III, Pages 123 – 166. Toronto Ontario Historical Society, 1901.

Pothier, Philippe, "POTHIER, TOUSSAINT," in *Dictionary of Canadian Biography*, vol. 7, University of Toronto/Université Laval, 2003–, accessed May 3, 2018, http://www.biographi.ca/en/bio/pothier_toussaint_7E.html.

Straus, Frank. *Forgotten army Captain Left Legacy on Mackinac Island.* Mackinac Island Town Crier, May 17, 2014.

Tasse, Joseph. *Les Canadiens de l'Ouest*. Montreal. Cie. Dimprimerie Canadienne. 1878.

www.ingramcontent.com/pod-product-compliance
Lightning Source LLC
Chambersburg PA
CBHW070535030426
42337CB00016B/2218